THINGS TO MAKE AND DO

Contents

LEAVES, PEBBLES AND MOSS

Plate Gardens

Wile away a rainy afternoon making a miniature garden. These realistic-looking gardens are laid out on dinner plates. You could create an imaginary garden or recreate a section of your own garden. Have a look around outside for plants and tiny flowers to use to decorate your plate garden. Make fences from lollysticks or twigs and use your imagination to help you create miniature copies of real life objects. Use tiny pebbles to make a garden path. See if you can find some miniature ornaments that will be the right scale for garden statues.

You will need:

Plate
Sand
Potting compost
Pebbles
Sticks and thread
Dried flowers and moss
Selection of leaves and flowers
Modelling clay
Salt
Scissors
Paper

1 Place a layer of sand on a plate and cover it with a layer of potting compost. Use small pebbles to lay a path. Make some beanpoles from twigs tied with thread and press them firmly into the earth.
Use some moss to create a hedge.

2 The garden is now ready for the vegetables to be 'planted'. A small leaved plant stem has been wound round the beanpoles, and a slightly larger leaved plant stem is laid on the earth. The carrot leaves are made from maidenhair fern with clay models of vegetables and garden tools laid amongst the leaves.

3 The washing is drying in a corner of this sweet little flower garden. Begin with a layer of sand on a plate and cover that with a thin layer of potting compost. Use some checked paper to make the path and two long twigs tied with a piece of string to make the washing line. A piece of paper is cut to make the white picket fence. Now cut some paper clothes to hang on the line.

4 The washing is hung on the line and the garden in now full of flowers and plants. Use moss as plants and some dried flowers pressed into the earth.

5 This winter scene is very effective. Place a layer of sand on the plate and make a snowman from modelling clay. Plant a few moss bushes and press some twigs into the sand. When your model is arranged pour salt over everything to create a snowscene.

Recycled Milk Cartons

Bird Feeders

Whether you live in the town or the country there will be wild birds about. You can easily attract the birds to your garden or windowsill by placing some wild bird seed in a small bird feeder where cats cannot get to it. The birds will enjoy a good feed and you will learn to recognize the different species. The bird feeder is made from an empty milk carton. If you hang it near a window you can keep an eye on the birds while you are out of sight, indoors. You might also want to thread some peanuts on a string and hang them out for the birds.

You will need:

Empty milk or juice carton
Scissors
Paint and paint-brush
Strong tape
String
Wild bird seed
Lard
Stale bread
Chopped apple and carrot
Small bowl
Saucepan
Spoon

1 Making this bird feeder is a good way to recycle a milk or juice carton. Cut away most of the sides of the carton leaving space at the base to hold the bird seed.

2 Once you have got the shape of the bird feeder right you can paint it. Choose a colour that will blend in with the surroundings and not frighten off the birds.

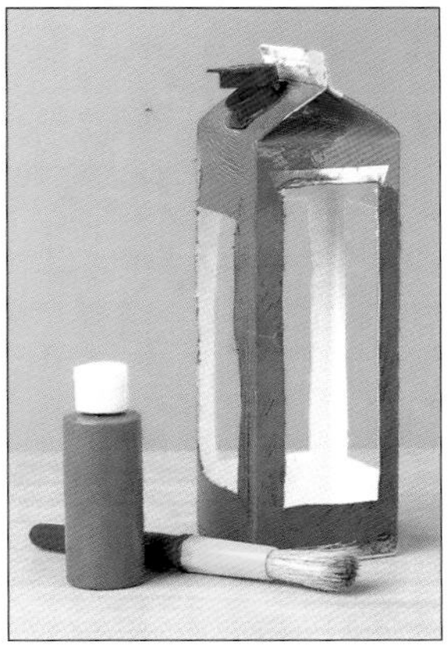

3 When the paint is dry you can decorate the bird feeder. Attach a piece of strong tape in a loop to the top of the feeder and fill the base with some wild bird seed.

4 Hang your bird feeder in a place, safe from the reach of cats. Thread some peanuts on a piece of string and hang that up alongside the feeder.

5 To make a bird seed ball you will need a saucepan and some lard, available from a supermarket. Melt the lard in a saucepan over a low heat (you may need an adult to help you with this). Collect the rest of your ingredients together. You can use old bread and wild bird seed and could always add some chopped carrot, assorted nuts or apple to the mixture.

6 Break a slice of bread into small pieces and place them in a bowl; pour over the melted lard. Add the wild bird seed and mix well together. As the mixture cools you will be able to form it into a ball. Push a piece of string into the centre of the mixture. Once it has hardened you will be able to hang the ball up with the string, alongside your bird feeder.

FLOWERS AND LEAVES

Pressed Flowers

Flower pressing was a popular activity among ladies in the nineteenth century. Nowadays flower pressing is regaining popularity as a hobby. If you have a garden it is easy to find flowers to press, although you should check with an adult before you pick any flowers. Pressing flowers dries them out, flattening them and leaving a little of the original colour. This creates a material you can use to decorate writing paper and greeting cards, and if you press enough flowers you could create a whole picture or cover a small box. Once you have pressed your flowers, store them flat between layers of tissue paper in a box in a dry, airy place to save their colour.

You will need:

Fresh picked flowers to press

Flower press or old book

Scissors

Glue

Items to decorate

When picking flowers to press make sure that they have no insects in them, and that the petals are perfect, not torn or brown.

Put the flowers in your flowerpress or in tissue between the pages of a thick book, as soon after picking as possible.

1 Pressing flowers is a wonderful hobby. Press the flowers flat in a flowerpress or use an old book. The flowers will need to be left in place for quite a few weeks before they are ready to use.

2 Pressed flowers can be used to decorate greeting cards. You can buy prepared cards to decorate or make your own from nice paper. Spend a little time trying out designs by laying different pressed flowers and leaves on the paper. When you are happy with your design use a little glue to attach the pressed flowers to the card. You may want to paint on a little varnish to give the picture a high gloss finish.

3 For a rose picture, press a whole rose carefully in your flowerpress. Leave it for a few weeks until most of the moisture has dried out. Choose a small frame and place the pressed rose in it. If you press lots of flowers you may have enough to cover a small box.

Veg, Meat and Fish

Burgers

Follow our easy recipes for burgers which are quick to prepare and delicious to eat. Make them from minced meat, cooked beans, tofu or fish. There is a recipe to suit every taste. For a professional look serve your burgers with a garnish such as a slice of lemon, cress or sliced tomato and lettuce.

You will need:

Ingredients

Bowl

Potato masher

Wooden spoon

Frying pan

Plates and cutlery to serve

Bean Burgers:

1 can of black-eyed beans

1 small chopped onion, fried

1 teaspoon mixed herbs

1 egg

1 cup of wholemeal breadcrumbs

Flour to roll the finished burgers in

A little oil for frying

Tofu Burgers:

250g block of tofu, chopped

1 small chopped onion, fried

2 teaspoons fresh or dried parsley

1 cup wholemeal breadcrumbs

2 teaspoons soya sauce

Sesame seeds to roll finished burgers in

A little oil for frying

Fish burgers:

155g tin pilchards in tomato sauce

1 cup wholemeal breadcrumbs

1 small chopped onion, fried

1 teaspoon mixed herbs

Flour to roll the finished burgers in

A little oil for frying

Lamb burgers:

250g minced lamb

1 teaspoon mixed herbs

salt and pepper to taste

1 egg

half a cup of wholemeal breadcrumbs

Flour to roll the finished burgers in

A little oil for frying

1 Empty the beans or other main ingredient into the bowl and mash them well.

2 Add the rest of the ingredients and mix well with a wooden spoon. Use your hands to shape the mixture into burger shapes and roll in flour.

3 Fry in a little hot oil, serve on a burger bun. A tasty meal, easily prepared.

Always have an adult in the kitchen when you are cooking on top of the stove.

Wash your hands before preparing food.

Peppermint and Chocolate

Sweets

You will need:

12 tablespoons of icing sugar
1 egg-white
Peppermint flavouring
Green food colouring
Wooden spoon
Bowl
Knife and board
Plain chocolate
Small bowl
Foil
Tray
Glacé cherries

Home-made sweets are fun to make and delicious to eat! Try your hand at chocolate-dipped peppermints or cherries. The fruit is made from marzipan and painted with food colouring. You may find that making them takes a little practice, but once you have mastered the art you could make a bowl of miniature marzipan fruit. Have a look at some real fruit for inspiration. Fresh fruit can also be dipped into chocolate – try it with some orange segments.

1 Place the icing sugar, egg-white, 4 drops peppermint flavouring, 12 drops green colouring into a bowl and mix well. You may need to add a little more icing sugar. Knead the mixture for a few minutes until it forms a smooth ball.

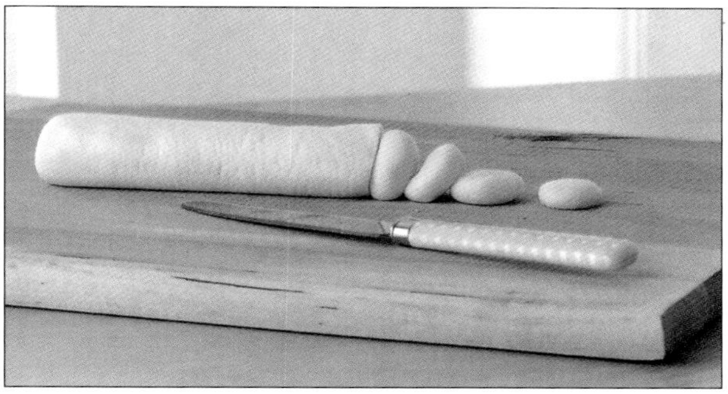

2 Form the mixture into a sausage shape and slice into discs. Use your hands to shape the discs into round sweet shapes and place on a board to dry.

3 Ask an adult to melt the chocolate in a small bowl. Dip the dry peppermints into the melted chocolate until they are half covered. Place the chocolate dipped peppermints on a foil-covered tray to set.

4 To make chocolate-dipped cherries, first wash the syrup off the glacé cherries. Pat them dry with kitchen towel and use a cocktail stick to dip them into the melted chocolate. Decorate the dipped cherries with a small piece of cherry.

Always wash your hands before you handle food.

Remember to tidy up as you go along.

Air hardening Clay

Egg Cups

Boiled eggs for breakfast will never be the same again with one of these fun egg cups. They are made from air-hardening clay. Make a Humpty Dumpty egg cup for a young brother or sister, or choose a more stylish crown or simple shape painted to match your breakfast plates. Make a set of egg cups, one for each member of the family, decorated to suit their hobbies or interests.

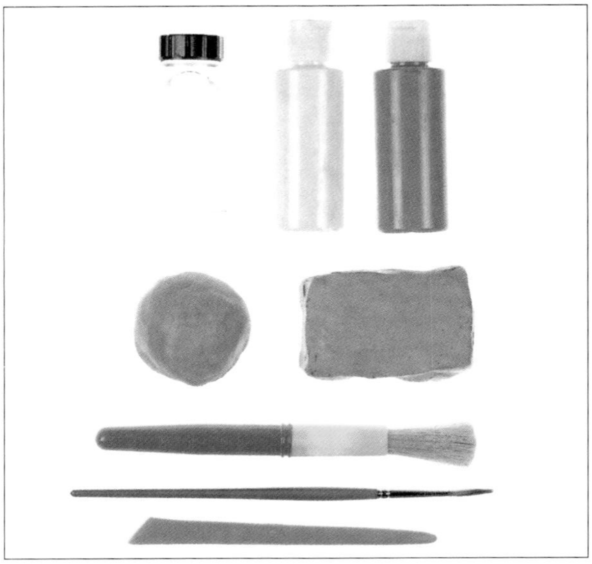

You will need:

A block of air hardening clay

Clay modelling tool

Tray to stand the egg cup on while it is drying

Acrylic paints

Paint-brush

Varnish

1 Begin by shaping a block of clay to be the wall for Humpty to sit on.

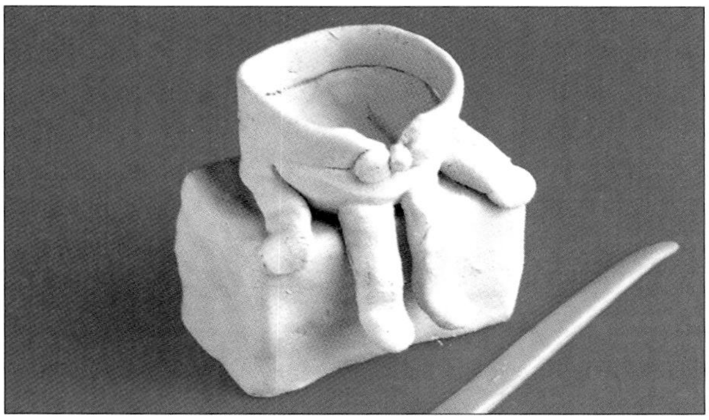

2 Make the legs and arms from sausage shapes and use an egg to gauge the size of the cup. Once you have made your model, leave it to dry for 24 hours.

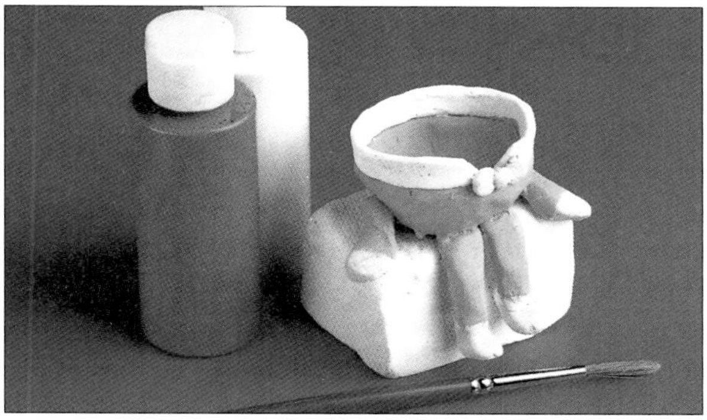

3 When the model is completely dry, you can decorate it. Paint one colour at a time allowing each shade to dry.

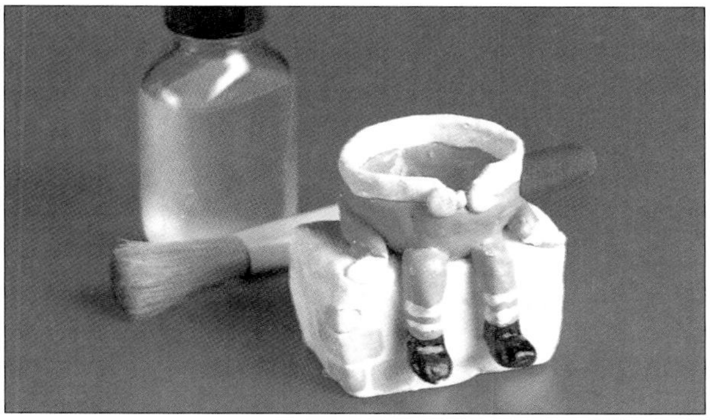

4 Varnish the egg cup when the paint is completely dry.

Before you begin, cover your work surface with newspaper or a plastic cloth – working with clay can be a messy business. It is a good idea to work on a tray which will enable you to carry your finished item to a safe place to dry.

If you cannot get hold of air hardening clay, make Humpty from salt and flour dough: mix 2 cups of plain flour and 1 cup of fine salt, add 1 cup of water and mix well. Knead for 5 minutes, then the dough will be ready for use.

PAPER AND CARD

Bookmarks

Bookmarks will always come in handy, whether you enjoy fairytales or mysteries. These bookmarks are made from thin card and coloured with felt tip pens. A bookmark made from your initial written in bubble writing and decorated with bright colours would take no time to make. You could take inspiration from the book you are reading or make one representing a particular hobby or interest.

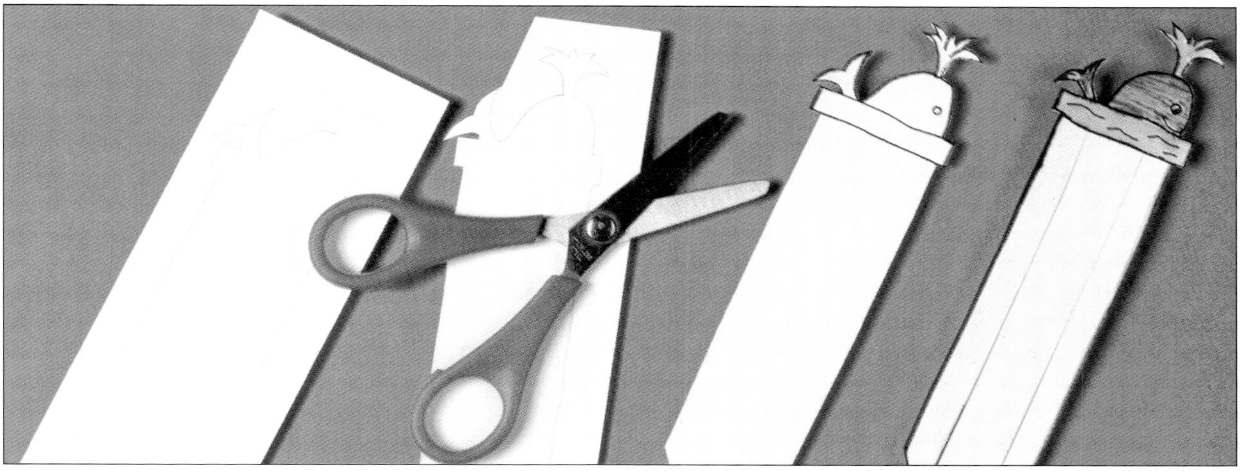

1 Use pencil to outline the whale. When you are happy with the shape cut it out.

Use felt tip pens to colour in the design and draw a neat border with a black felt tip pen.

2 Personalise your bookmark by using your initial. Draw the outline in pencil first, then go over it with a felt tip pen before you decorate the inner part of the initial.

3 This bookmark would look good in a gardening book!

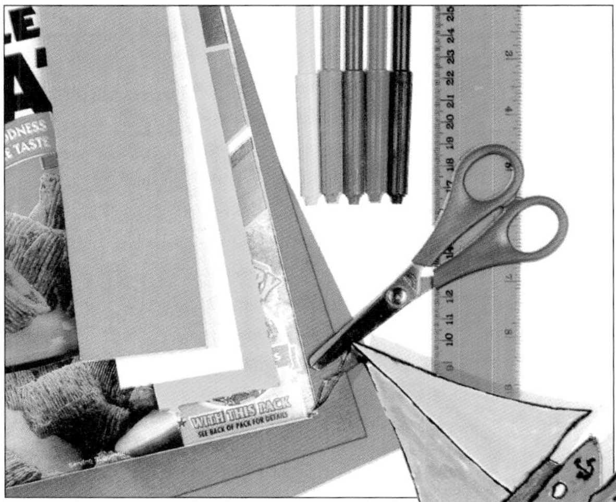

You will need:

Thin card
Pencil
Scissors
Felt tip pens

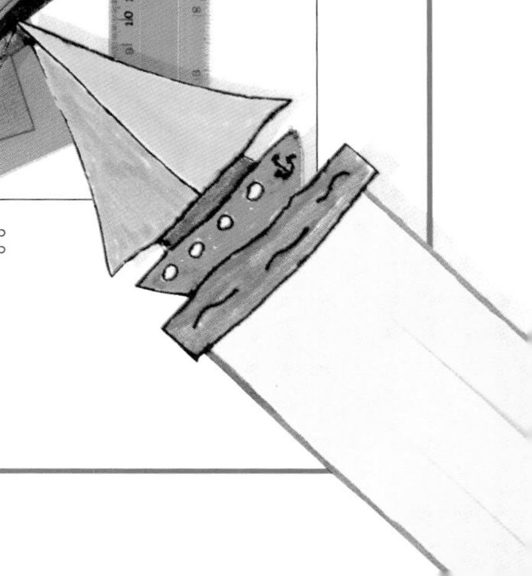

CARD AND PAPER

Teddy Bears

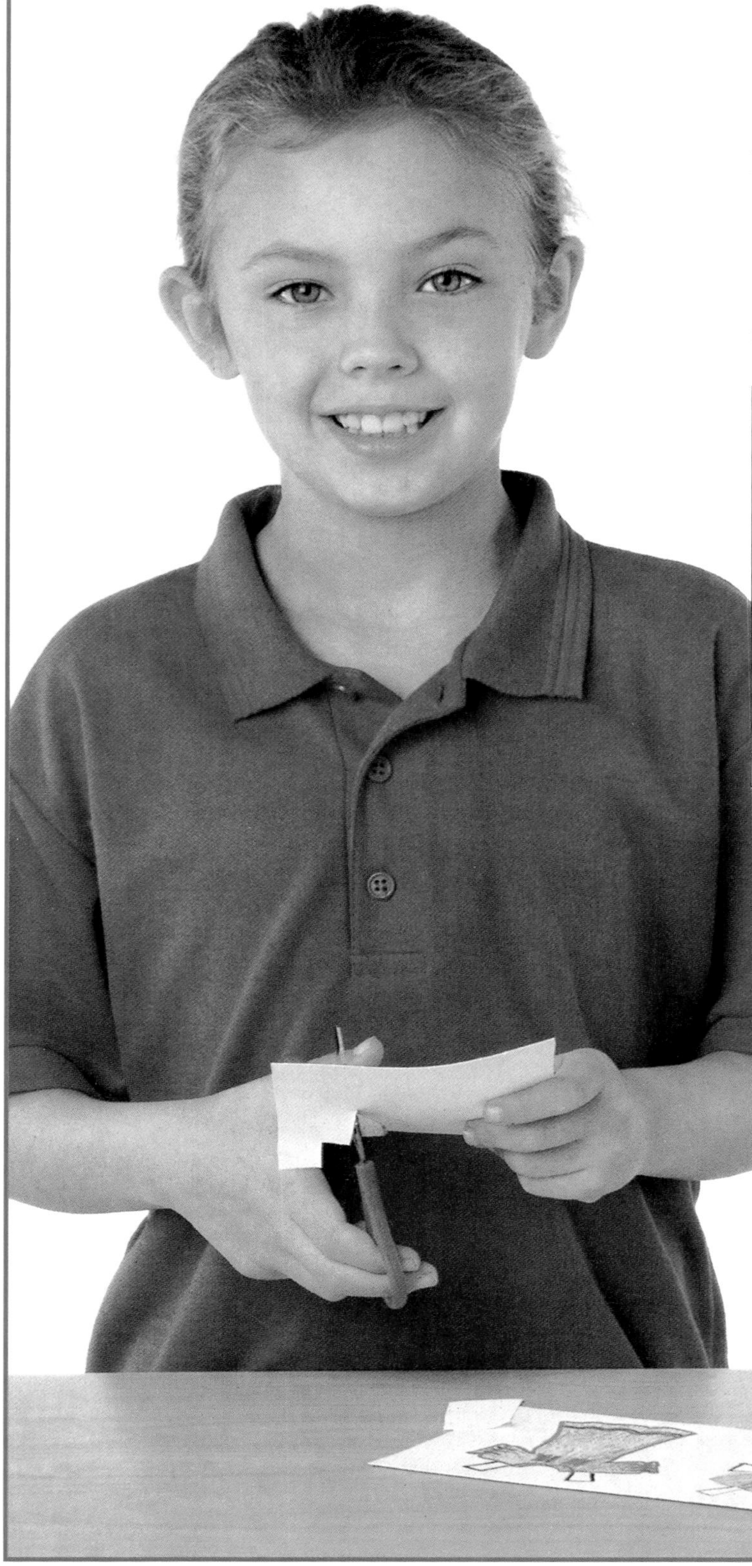

Make a whole family of cut-out bears and design outfits for them - playclothes, fancy dress, pyjamas. These bears are drawn on thin, white card and coloured with pencil crayons. If you do not have any card to hand, use card cut from a cereal or tea box to make the bears and their outfits. A simple folded bed would be fun to decorate.

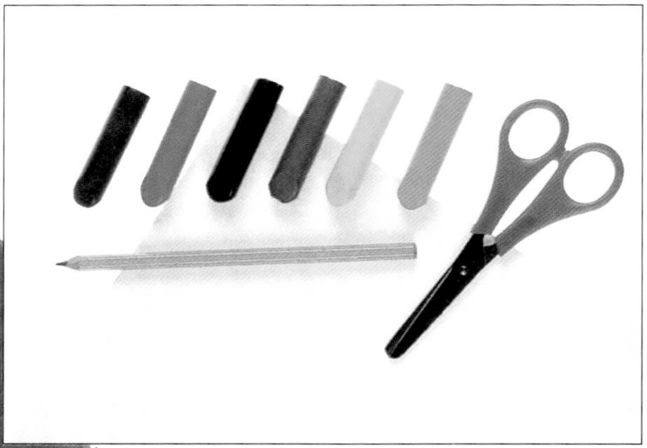

You will need:

Thin card or stiff paper

Pencil

Crayons

Scissors

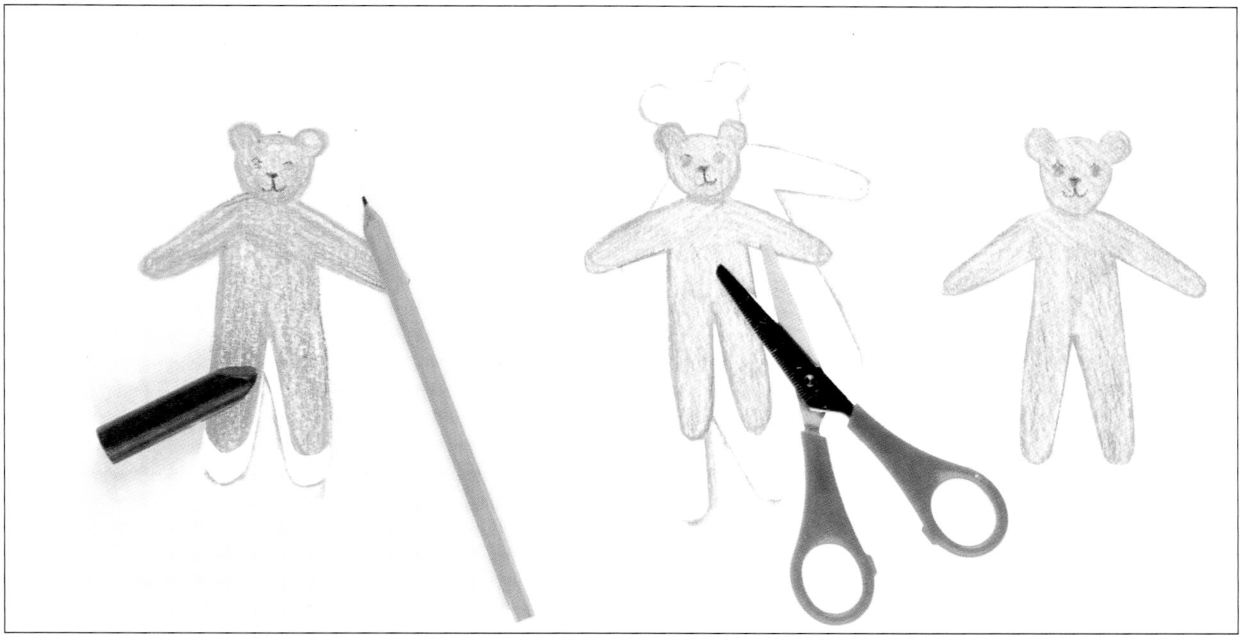

1 Draw a teddy bear onto thin card. Give it a face and colour it in using bright crayon colours. Cut it out. Make several members of a teddy bear family to dress.

2 Lay the cut-out teddy bears onto paper or thin card and draw an outfit around each shape. Fill in and colour.

Remember to tidy away all the scraps of paper and card when you have made your cut-out bears.

Felt

Beads

Turn ethnic-looking beads made from coloured felt into great chokers, bracelets and pendants. The beads are made from layers of felt glued or tied together. They are threaded on embroidery silk. Make a selection of colours and shapes and combine them with wooden beads to make an exotic necklace.

You will need:

Felt squares (from a craft shop)

Scissors

Fabric glue

Elastic band

Needle and coloured thread

Small quantity of stuffing

Ribbon

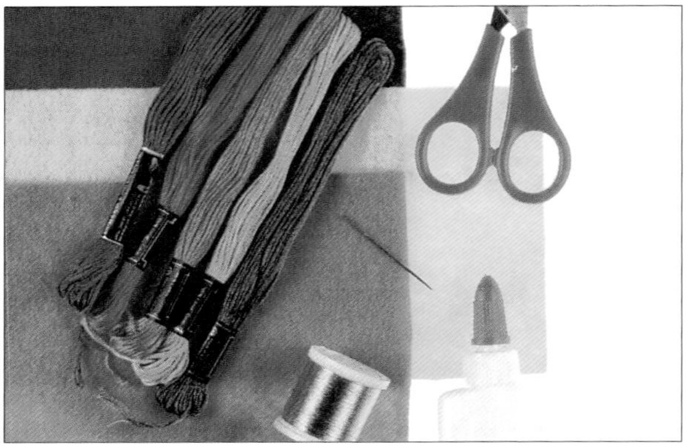

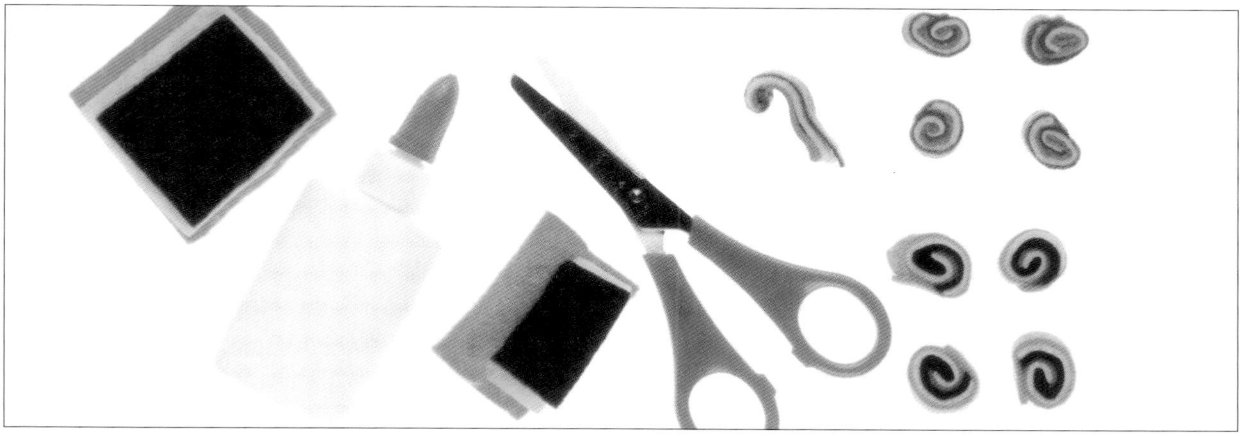

1 Cut three squares of coloured felt, each slightly smaller than the other. Layer them, using a little glue to hold them in place. Now roll them tightly in a sausage shape and hold in place with glue. You may need to wind a little thread around them or hold them in place with an elastic band. The glue will need to dry thoroughly. When the glue has set, use scissors to cut the sausage into beads.

2 You will need two squares of coloured felt. Cut out a heart shape from each colour, with one heart slightly smaller than the other. Place a little stuffing between the layers and sew them together with coloured thread. Make a ribbon loop at the top of the heart for threading.

3 Roll up a small square of felt. Hold the roll in place with glue. Wind coloured thread around the sausage-shaped felt pieces to make decorative bands.

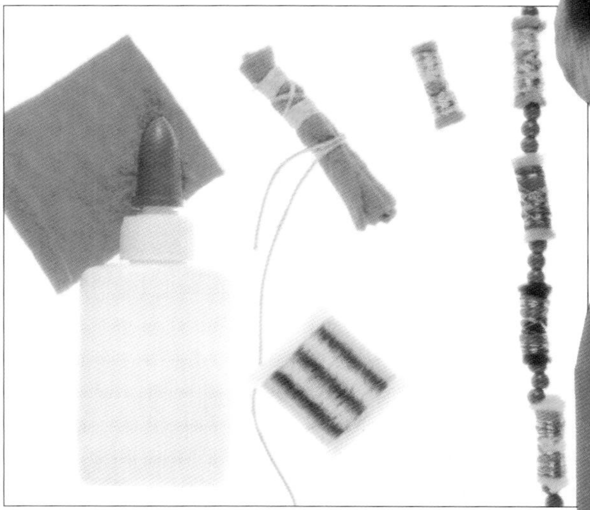

THIN CARD AND PAPER

Pop-up Cards

This pop-up card is simple to make and will brighten up someone's day. When placed on a windowsill or mantlepiece it will look as if a bunch of flowers is bursting out of the card. The cards are made and decorated with thin card. If you don't have any coloured thin card available, use card from a cereal packet and paint it in bright colours yourself.

You will need:

Coloured thin card

Scissors

Glue

Coloured paper

Felt tips pens

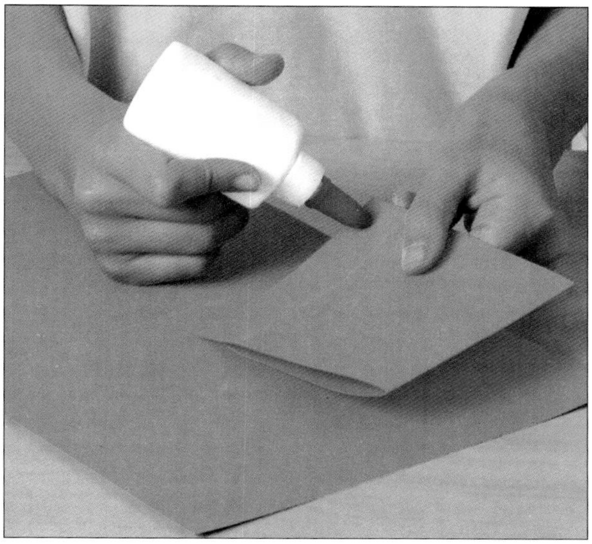

1 Begin by folding a sheet of thin card in half and then open it out. Cut out a small square of card and fold it in half. Fold a lip on the two edges, and glue these into the card to make the vase. Open and close the card to check the vase flattens when you close it.

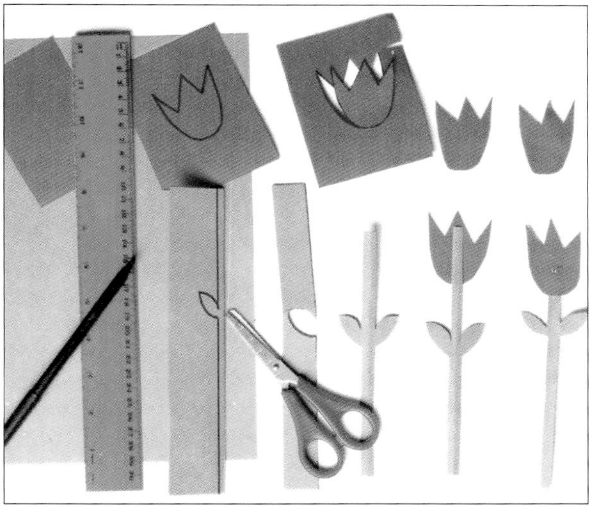

2 Using green thin card, cut the stalks and leaves, use glue to attach these to the inside of the vase. Cut out some tulip-shaped flowers and glue them onto the stalks, making sure that they are hidden when the card is closed.

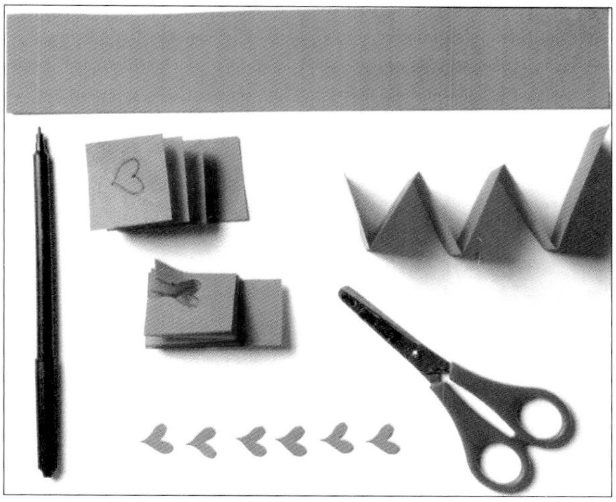

3 Cut small heart shapes to decorate the vase from red paper, folded over.

4 Now decorate the front of the card with a large red heart and a smaller blue heart, to match the rest of the design. Now you are ready to write your message on the card, using felt tip pens.

When trying out something for the first time, start by making a rough example out of scrap paper and card.

RIBBONS AND THREAD

Bows & Ribbons

Bows and ribbons provide the final touch to a beautifully wrapped gift. You can decorate plain ribbon with felt tip pens, creating your own designs. The ribbons shown here are decorated with tiny motor vehicles and balloons, but any design would be fun. Hallowe'en pumpkins or Christmas trees are bright and easy to draw. Bows are quick to make using the method shown. Choose thin ribbon to make small bows and wider ribbon for larger bows. Co-ordinate the patterns and colours of your home made bows with wrapping paper for a stylish look.

You will need:

Ribbon

Felt tip pens

Ruler

Scissors

Needle and thread

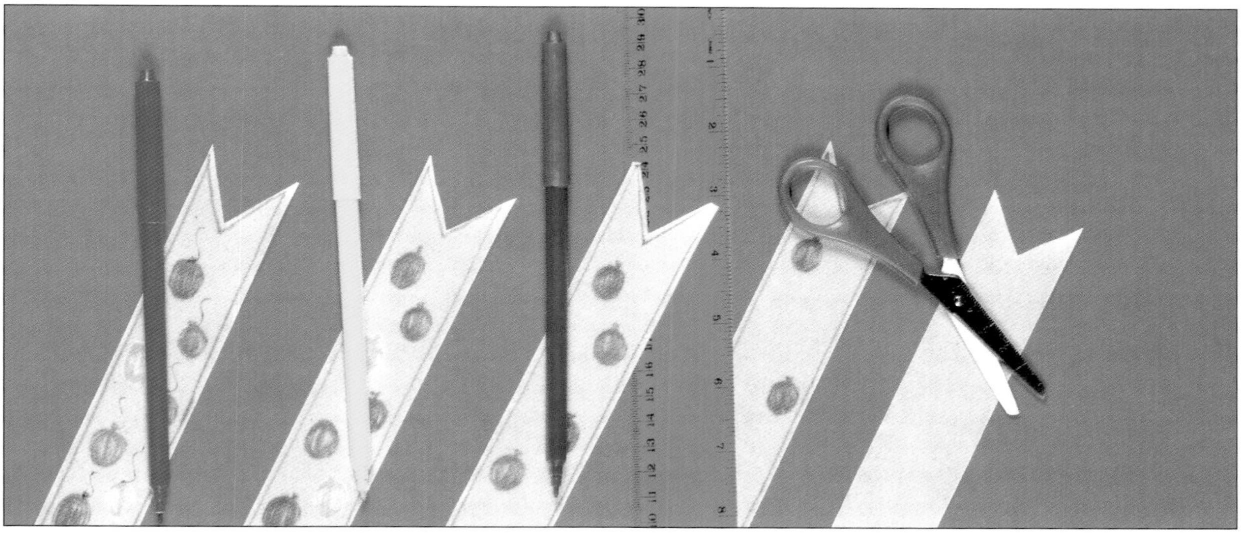

1 Use felt tip pens to decorate plain ribbon. Cut a little ribbon off to practise on. Press the pen down gently to prevent the colour bleeding across the weave of the ribbon. Complete the use of one colour before moving on to the next. Remember to repeat your pattern to give the ribbon a shop bought look.

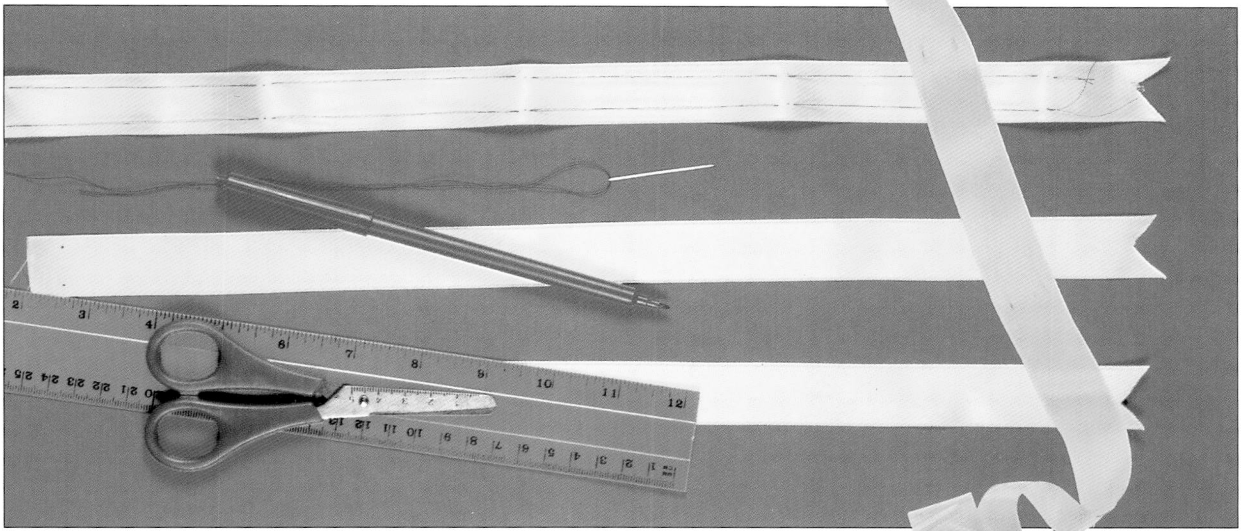

2 Spread a 60cm length of ribbon across the work surface. Use a felt tip pen and ruler to make a tiny mark every 6cm. Thread the needle with thread about 20cm longer than the ribbon and make a good knot at the end. Sew a small stitch at each mark on the ribbon. Now pull gently at the thread and the ribbon should bunch up, making a fancy bow.

PAPER

Printed Cards

Spend a rainy afternoon making potato cuts to print with and you will be able to set up a production line and make a collection of cards or writing paper. The fish card is made with layers of different coloured paper, each slightly smaller than the other. Biscuit cutters come in lots of shapes and provide a quick way to make home made stamps. Use a small rabbit shape to decorate writing paper and envelopes. The bunch of carrots is made by first drawing the shape onto the potato half, then cutting it out with a knife. A set of cards tied with matching ribbon would make a good gift.

You will need:

A potato

Biscuit cutters

Knife

Paint and saucer

Sponge

Paper

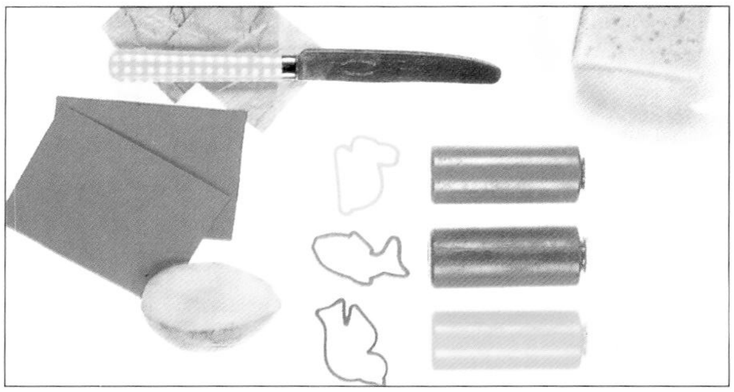

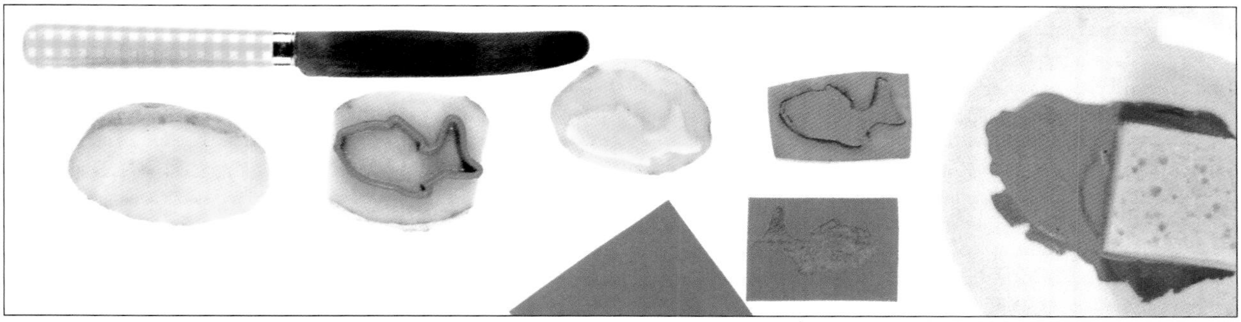

1 Begin by cutting a potato in half. Take the fish-shaped biscuit cutter and press it firmly into the flesh of one half of the potato. Use the knife to cut around the shape. Lift off the cutter and remove the excess potato flesh. Put a little paint onto a saucer and use the sponge to evenly distribute the paint on the stamp. Now press the stamp gently onto blue paper. Print a few fish and leave them to dry.

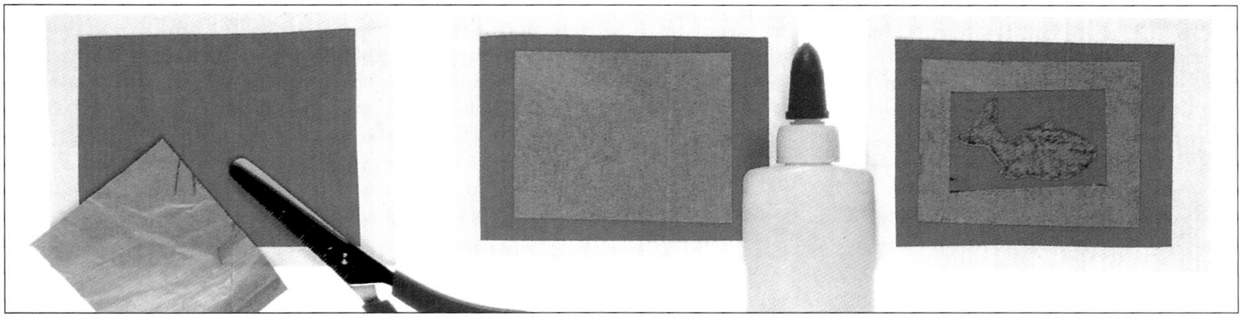

2 Take a white sheet of paper and fold it in half to make the card. Now take a square of blue paper slightly smaller than the card and glue it on the front. Next glue on a small piece of gold paper. Cut out the fish print and glue it on top.

3 To finish off the picture you will need to make a simple stamp from the other half of the potato. Use the knife to cut a weed shape. Spread green paint on the stamp and print leaves of seaweed onto the card. Leave to dry.

Protect your work surface with newspaper or a plastic cloth before you begin.

It is a good idea to practise stamping your design on some scrap paper to get an idea of how much paint you need to apply to the stamp.

FABRIC PAINT

Beach Shoes

Beach shoes are very useful, but usually come in rather dull black or white. Use fabric paints to decorate them. The fabric paints used in this project are available from craft and fabric shops and are easy to use. It is a good idea to practise first on a piece of card. Try out a few designs. Fish or flowers make good patterns. Choose a pattern that is easy to repeat.

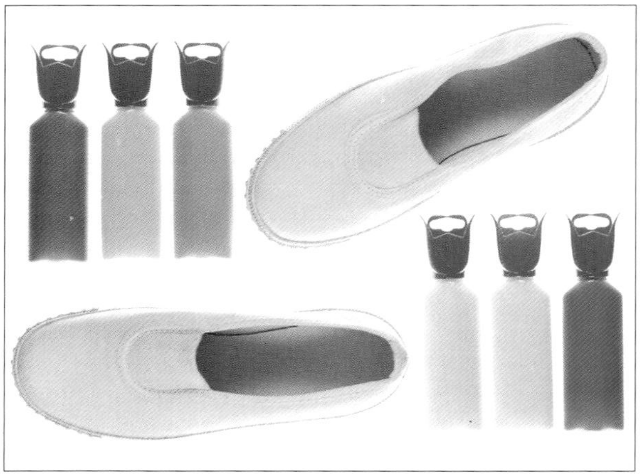

You will need:

Canvas shoes

Fabric paint

Be sure to clean up any spills as they occur. Don't forget to leave your work area tidy.

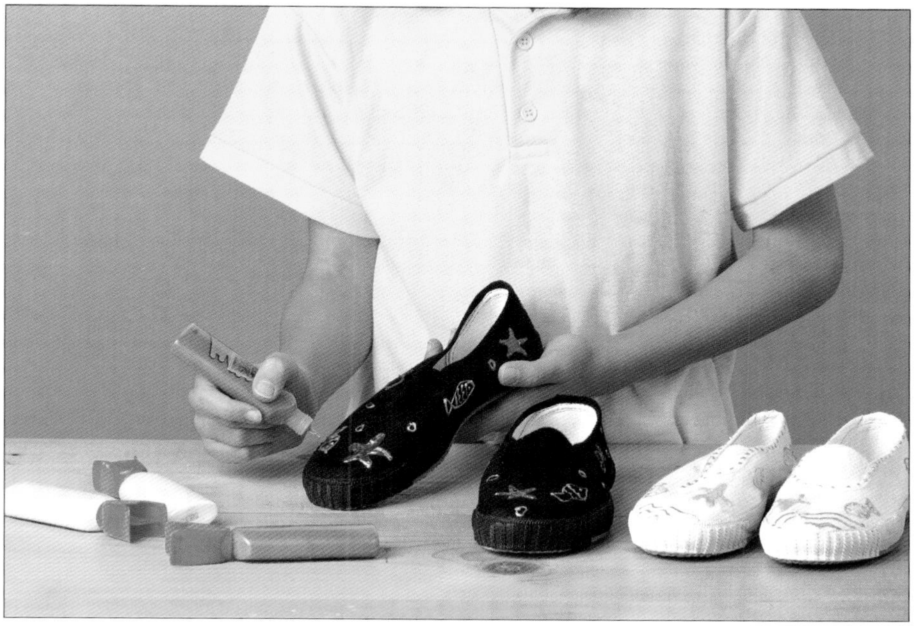

1 These shoes have been painted with a seaside theme. Take care not to smudge the decoration as you go along. When you have completed the first shoe use it as a pattern for the other one. In that way you will be able to create a matching design. Once your shoes are decorated leave them in a safe place to dry completely before you wear them on your next beachcombing expedition.

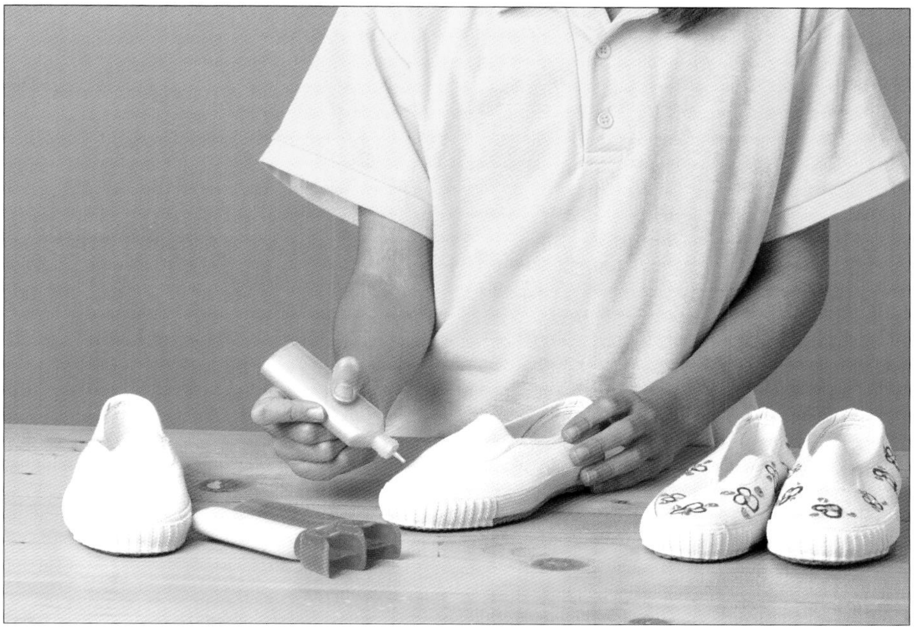

2 Flower patterns are easy to draw on and look very attractive. Decorate a pair of shoes to wear during the summer months. You could take inspiration from a special dress or T-shirt.

Plaster-of-Paris and Air Hardening Clay

Lighthouse

Models are great fun to make. This lighthouse standing on a rocky island surrounded by the blue sea looks very realistic. Spend some time planning your model, then make a rough drawing. If you have been to the seaside you may recall a particular lighthouse or other seaside scene which you could re-create in miniature. When you are away on holiday you may want to collect a few pebbles and some sand to use to make the model when you return home. It is amazing what you can achieve with some plaster, pebbles and paint.

You will need:

A cardboard lid
Margarine tub
Stones
Pebbles
Plaster-of-Paris
Bowl and spatula
Air hardening clay
Glue
Paint and paint-brushes

1 Place the margarine tub towards one end of the box lid. Position the stones; they will jut out of the 'water' so need to be quite tall. When you are happy with the arrangement mix up the plaster-of-Paris in the bowl and pour it over everything.

2 You will now need to make the lighthouse. Use some air hardening clay and make a long cylinder shape, wider at one end than the other. The room at the top will need to be made separately. Leave the pieces to dry in a warm airy spot.

3 When the plaster and the lighthouse pieces are dry you can glue everything in place. Use strong glue. Leave the model in a warm airy spot to dry.

4 Spread a thick layer of glue where ever you need to place the small pebbles. These will give the impression of rocks. A few on top of the island will look good.

5 Once your model is dry it is ready to paint and decorate. Have fun and use plenty of imagination to create a realistic-looking rocky, seaside scene.

PLASTIC CONTAINERS AND OVEN BAKE CLAY

Skittles

Enjoy a game of skittles whenever you like with these brightly decorated recycled drink containers. You will need six containers to make a set. Paint them in bright colours and decorate them with coloured stars. If they get knocked over too easily, pour some sand into each one to make them heavier. Mini- or table-skittles can also be fun. You could make a set to take away on holiday. They are made from oven bake clay. Take turns with a friend to see how many skittles you can knock down with each shot.

You will need:

Empty drink containers

Paint

Paint-brushes

Sand, for weight

To make mini-skittles you will need:

Oven bake clay

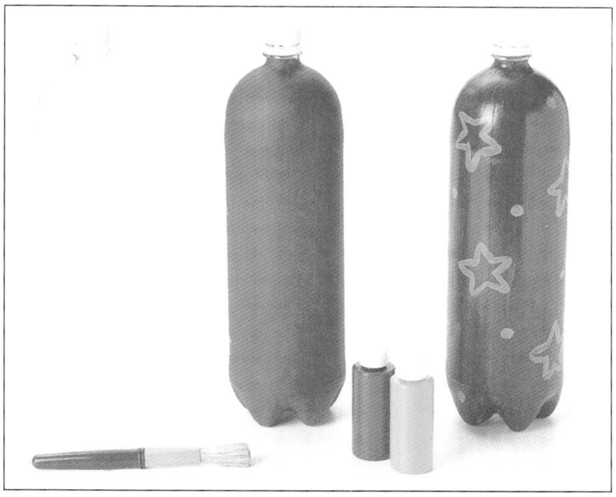

1 Wash out the drink containers well. Leave upside down to drain. Screw the lids on tightly and your skittles are ready for painting. Begin by painting a base coat.

You may need two layers of paint. When the base coat is dry, paint on the decoration. When all your skittles are painted and decorated they are ready for use.

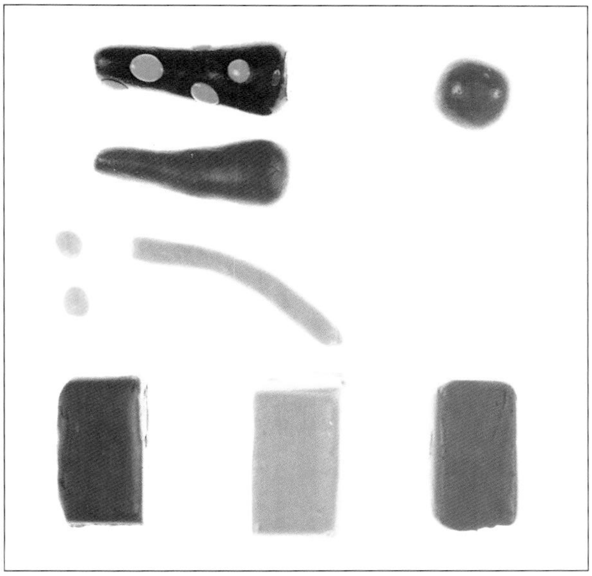

2 To make these mini-skittles you will need oven bake clay in three colours. Divide the clay into equal pieces and shape the skittles. Use oven bake clay of a different colour to make flattened ball shapes and press them onto the skittles. Shape a ball and when your ball and skittles are ready, bake in the oven according to the manufacturer's directions. You might want to decorate a small box in which to store your mini-skittles.

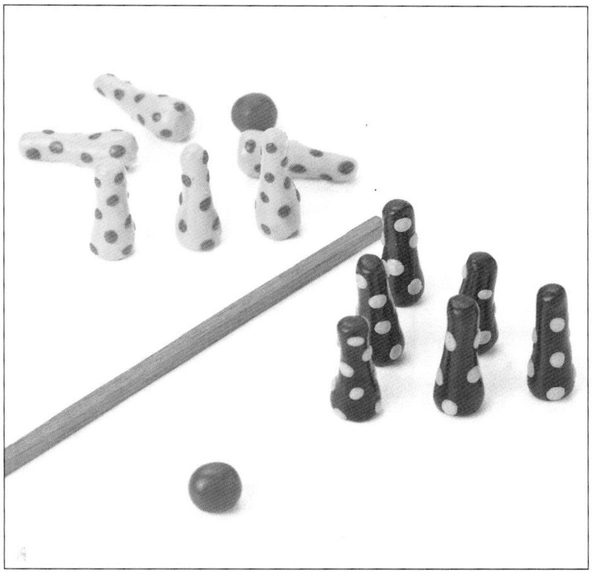

A set of mini-skittles would make a good Christmas cracker gift or party favour.

A full size set of skittles could be used at a school games day or fund raising event.

Plastic and Paper

Magic Pictures

This fishy picture changes from black and white to colour quite magically. Make one to delight a younger brother or sister. Choose your picture carefully: an empty black and white hillside could turn into a green pasture covered with sheep, or a bare table top could have a birthday cake appear on it. Use brightly coloured felt tip pens to colour your picture. It is a good idea to keep the shapes simple. If you don't have a plastic folder you might be able to recycle a piece of clear plastic from a carton.

You will need:

Thin card or paper

Scissors

Marker and felt tip pens

Plastic folder

Sticky tape

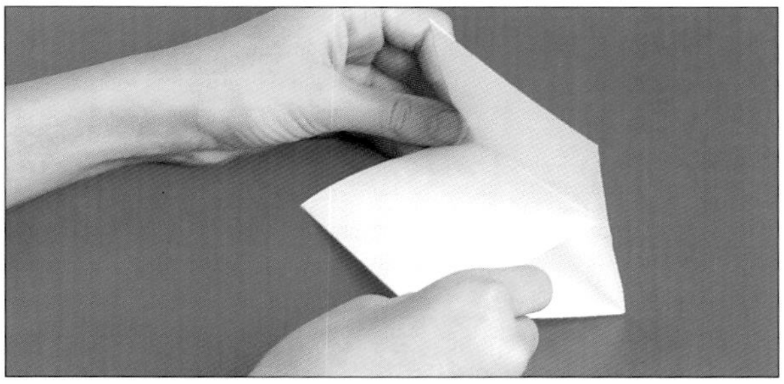

1 Take a sheet of thin card or paper and fold it carefully into three equal sections as shown in the picture.

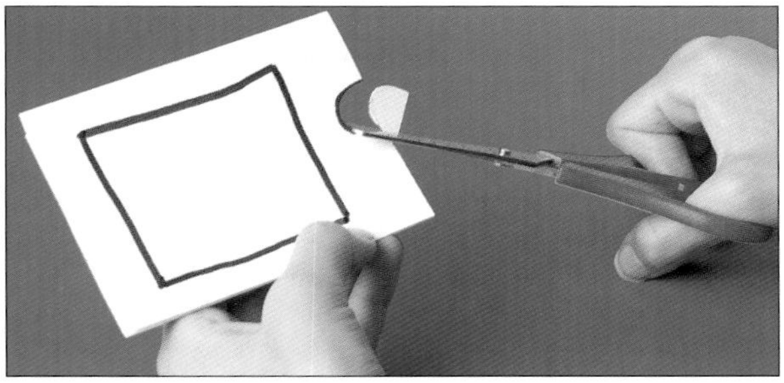

2 On the front flap mark out a rectangle and the finger grip space. Cut away the finger grip space.

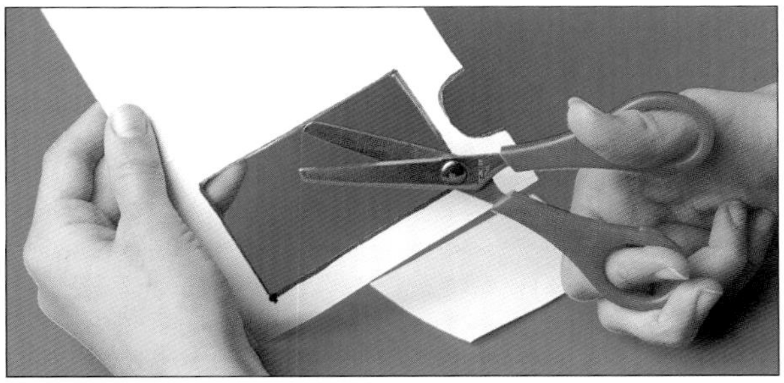

3 Open out the card and cut out the rectangle. This is the front of the card.

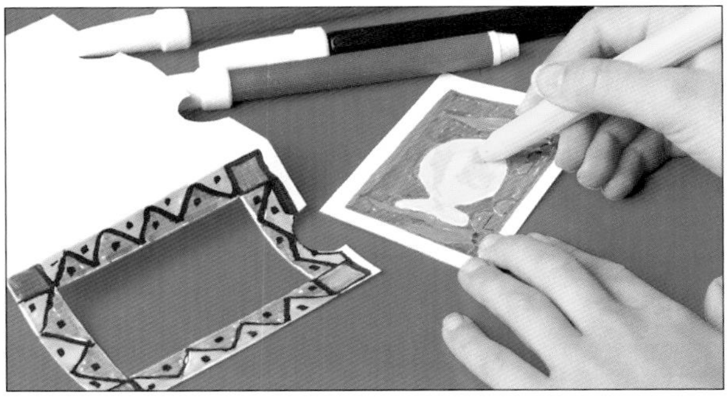

4 Draw a decorative border on this front frame. Cut a separate piece of paper the same size as one section of the card and draw on your design, using felt tip pens.

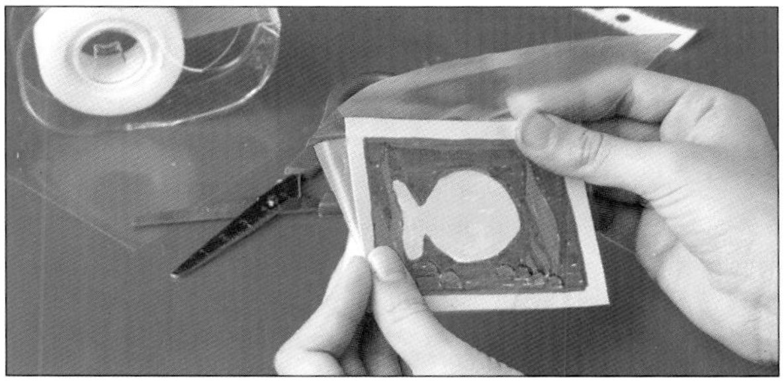

5 Slip your picture into the plastic folder with the top against a fold. Trim the plastic to the picture. Stick the back to the plastic.

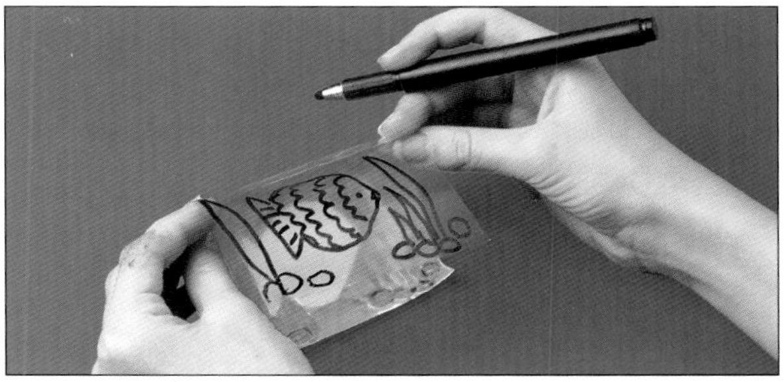

6 Use a marker pen to draw an outline of the picture on the plastic. Now take your card and open it out flat.

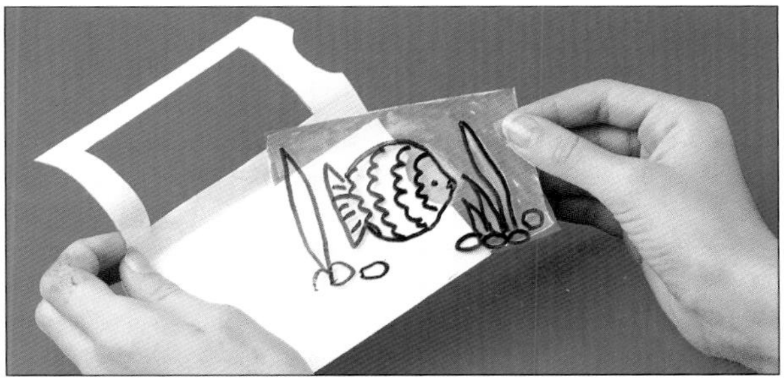

7 Fold the bottom flap into the middle. Slip the plastic-covered picture over the bottom flap. The bottom flap is now between the coloured picture and the outlined picture on the plastic flap. Fold the top flap down over the plastic. Grip the plastic and paper and pull; the picture will appear in colour as you pull it out.

SHOEBOX
Doll's House

Make a cute little doll's house for a miniature doll or bear to live in. This house is made from two boxes. Use any card you may have over to make miniature furniture. You may want to have a look round for some small matchboxes or other containers to recycle as furniture. Coloured paper makes good wallpaper, as does wrapping paper. Use a piece of fabric to make carpets and rugs, and don't forget some pictures to go on the walls. Decorate the outside of your house with paint, creating a cheerful summery scene for your doll to live in.

You will need:

Two shoeboxes
Scissors
Tape & glue
Large paper clips
Paint & paint-brushes
Paper & card
Small boxes
Felt tip pens

1 Use one of the boxes to make the house. Cut a corner off the other box to make the roof and cut the lid so that it fits inside the house as the upstairs floor.

2 Place the shoe box that will be the house up on one end. Use tape to attach the roof piece you have prepared at an angle to the top of the house. Use glue and tape to stick the floor section into place. Hold the floor in position with the large paperclips while the glue is setting.

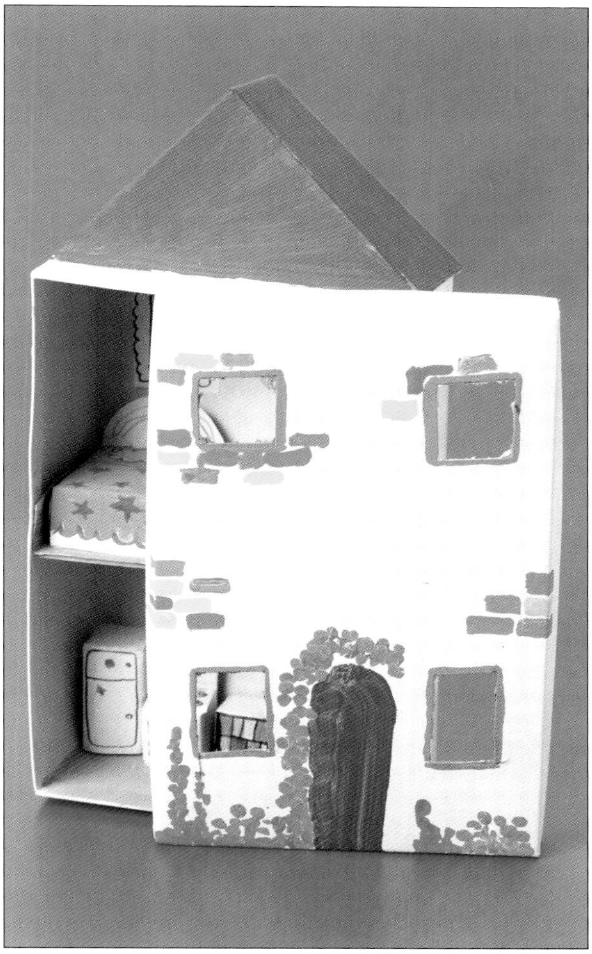

3 When the glue is set your house is ready to decorate. Paint the roof a rich reddy brown and the walls pale pink. Make a front for the house from the other shoebox lid and cut out windows. Paint a bright front door and flowers and make your house summery and cheerful.

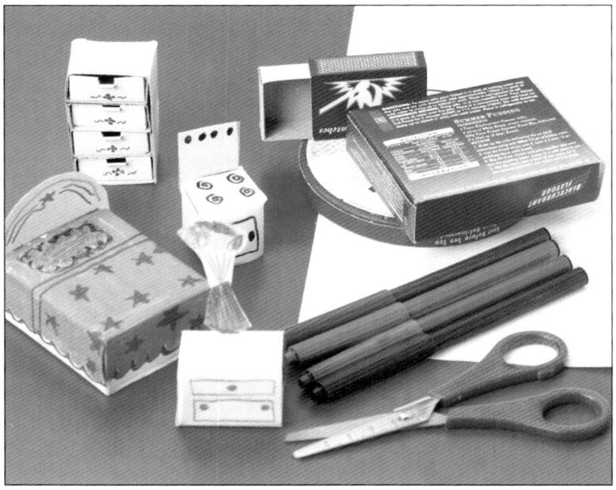

4 Miniature furniture is easy to make from scraps of paper and small boxes. Cover boxes with white paper to make kitchen equipment and coloured paper for furniture in other rooms. Use felt tip pens to outline shapes and decorate the pieces. Don't forget wallpaper and rugs and maybe some pictures on the walls.

THICK CARD

Jewellery Box

Keep your jewellery safe in one of these sparkling treasure troves. The boxes are made from thick card and decorated with gold and silver paint, glitter, glass beads and recycled junk jewellery. If you don't have any suitable old jewels, use brightly decorated gold or silver buttons or sequins.

You will need:

Thick card
Scissors
Sticky tape and glue
Newspaper
Gold paint and glitter
Shiny buttons or jewellery to recycle

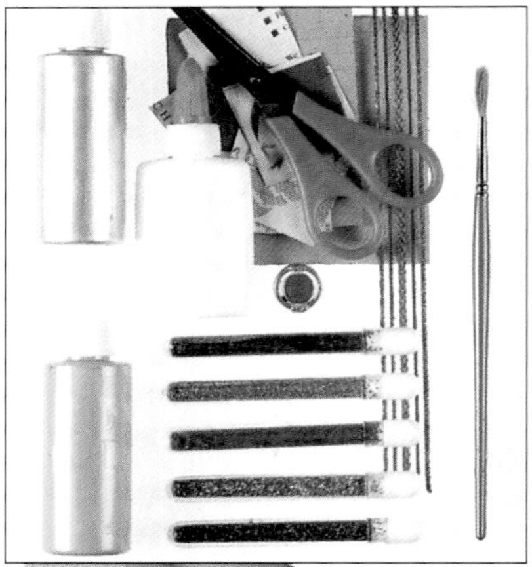

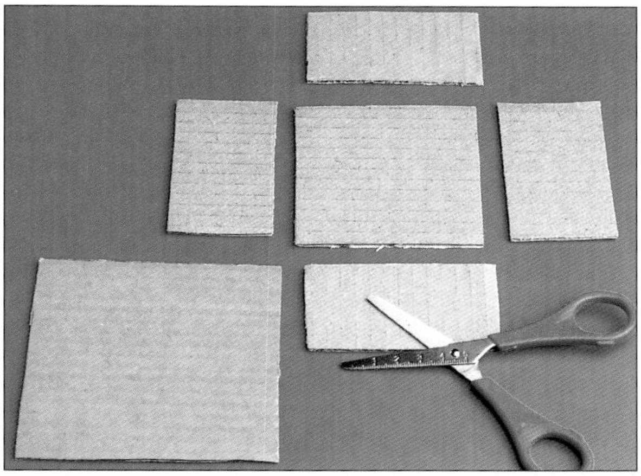

1 Cut a base and lid from thick card. Use the base to measure the size of the walls of the box.

2 Stick the shapes together to form the box. Use glue or sticky tape.

Remember to protect the work surface with newspaper before you begin.

3 Glue two layers of squares cut from the newspaper onto the box and lid. Leave in a warm airy spot to dry.

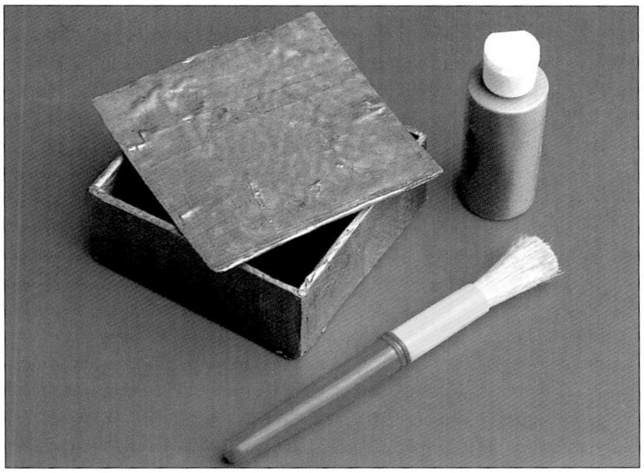

4 When the papier mâché layer is dry, it is ready to decorate. Paint the box inside and out with gold paint. It may need two coats. When the paint is dry, decorate the lid with glitter, paint and jewels.

MATCHBOX

Chest of Drawers

The decorations on these tiny chests of drawers give you a good idea of the contents. The chests of drawers are useful for storing stamps or buttons and are made from empty matchboxes, covered with sticky-backed paper. You may want to make a set of drawers for the toolbox to store small nails and screws. The button drawers would be good for saving odd buttons from the sewing box and stamp collectors would find the stamp drawers very useful. You could even make a tiny chest of drawers and decorate it to put in the doll's house bedroom.

You will need:

Empty matchboxes

Glue

Scissors

Sticky-backed paper

Felt

Selection of buttons and stamps

Thin wire (fuse wire would do well)

Saucer of water

Paper fasteners

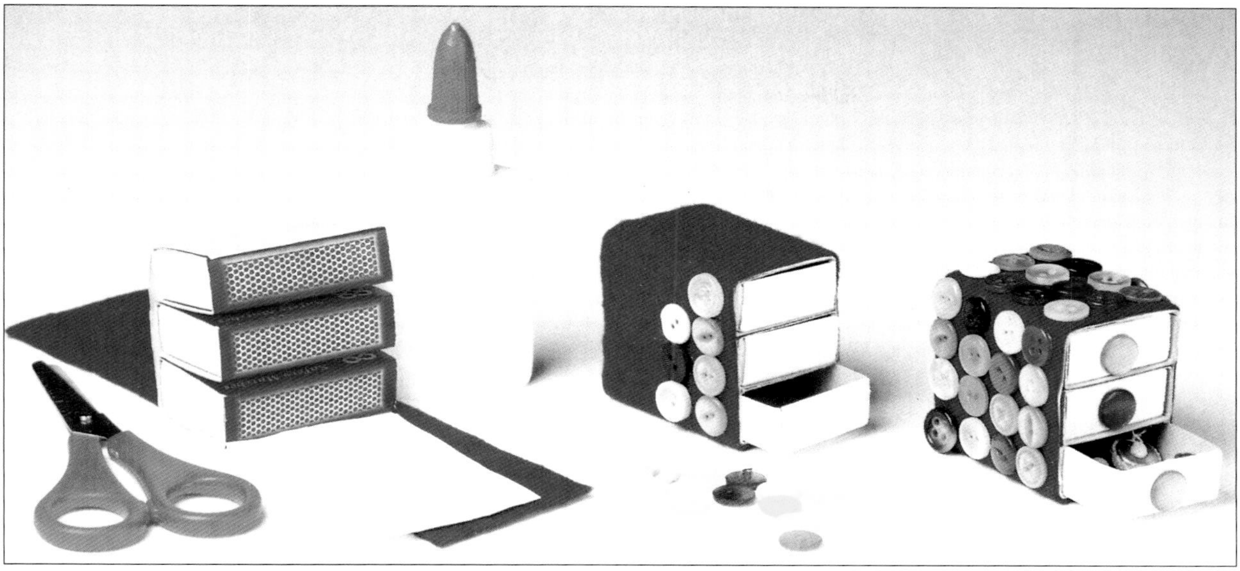

1 To make the button storage drawers, begin by gluing the three matchboxes, one on top of another. When the glue has dried, cover the set of drawers with sticky-backed paper. Spread the box with glue, then stick on the felt covering. Dab on a little glue and stick on the buttons, one at a time. To make handles for the drawers, attach buttons with a little wire.

2 To make the stamp drawer you will need a selection of brightly decorated stamps. Place the stamps in a saucer of water for a few minutes to loosen the glue and remove them from the envelope paper. Glue three matchboxes one on top of another then cover the box with sticky-backed paper. Glue on the stamps, taking care to arrange them so you can see the interesting pictures on them. Make drawer handles from paper fasteners.

You could use stickers to decorate a chest of drawers or decorate the sticky-backed paper with felt tip pens.

CAKES

Special Days

These novelty cakes look great on a party table and would make a surprise birthday gift to take to a party. The icing is simply rolled out with a rolling pin then placed over the cake. The decorative pieces are cut using biscuit cutters which come in so many shapes and sizes you are sure to find one to suit the style of cake you want to make. Use a bought-in sponge cake to ice or make your own. Ask an adult for help when you use the cooker.

1 Sieve some icing sugar onto your work surface so that the icing doesn't stick to it and roll out the icing to about half a centimetre thickness.

2 Roll the icing over the rolling pin and, lifting it gently, transfer it to the cake. Drape it over the cake and carefully remove the rolling pin.

3 Gently press the icing over the cake. Cut away any excess icing with a knife. Use a clean cloth to wipe away any icing sugar.

4 Roll out some red icing and use a biscuit cutter to cut out the star shapes. Moisten the back of the stars with a little water and press them gently onto the iced cake.

5 Use different shaped biscuit cutters to create different styles of cake. Green frogs, red stars or blue fish could be cut out and decorated further with silver balls or edible felt tip colours. Have fun creating your own designs to suit different occasions.

You will need

Sponge cakes to ice

Icing sugar

Rolling pin

Easy-roll icing

Knife

Clean cloth

Small sieve

Biscuit cutters

A little water and a pastry brush

HEART SHAPED BISCUITS AND FRAMES

St. Valentine's Day

You will need a heart shaped biscuit cutter to make both the picture frames and the gingerbread hearts! Both will make great Valentine gifts to give to friends and sweethearts. The gingerbread biscuits are simple to make and can be decorated with icing or left plain. Either way they are delicious to eat. The heart shaped picture frame has space for two pictures. It is made by rolling out the clay and using two biscuit cutters to cut the frame, one smaller than the other. A coat of varnish (or clear nail polish) will give your picture frame a professional finish.

You will need:

Air hardening clay
Heart biscuit cutter
Red paint
Paint-brush
Thread or ribbon
Glue

Recipe for gingerbread biscuits

350g plain flour
1 teaspoon baking powder
2 teaspoons ground ginger
1 teaspoon cinnamon
100g margarine
175g soft brown sugar
3 tablespoons syrup
1 egg
Icing

1 Place the flour, baking powder, ginger, cinnamon and sugar in a large bowl. Add the margarine, mix it in well with your fingertips until the mixture looks crumbly like breadcrumbs.

2 Add the sugar and syrup, mix together. Use a spoon to stir in the egg and mix.

3 Turn the mixture out onto the work surface and knead the mixture until it is smooth and well mixed. Sprinkle some flour onto the work surface and use the rolling pin to roll the mixture out to a thickness of about half a centimetre. With a heart shaped biscuit cutter cut out the shapes. Place the shapes on a baking tray and bake at 170°C, 325°F, gas mark 3 for just 10 minutes. Get an adult to help you use the oven.

4 When the gingerbread biscuits are cooked take them out of the oven and leave to stand until cold. They will harden up as they cool. When they are cool, decorate the biscuits with icing.

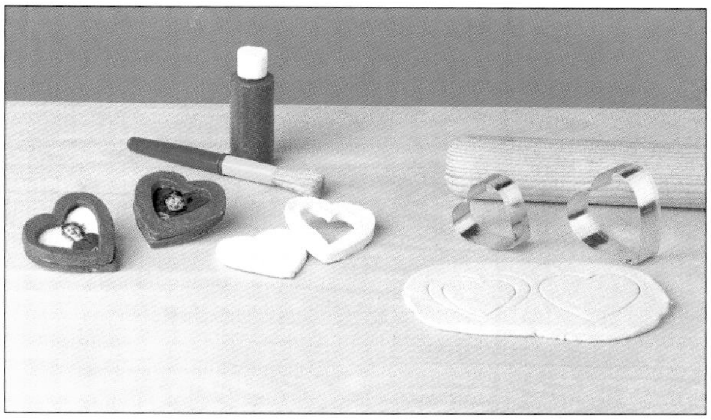

5 To make these picture frames you will need two biscuit cutters, one smaller than the other, and some air hardening clay. Roll out the clay and cut out two large heart shapes. One of the heart shapes will be the picture frame back. Take the smaller heart shaped biscuit cutter and cut a small heart shape out of the second heart shape. Leave the made frame pieces to dry in a warm airy place. When they have dried completely, paint them with red paint and glue them together. Place a picture of your Valentine in the frame. Use glue to secure it to the frame.

The heart-shaped frames look good enough to eat, but remember they are made from air hardening clay and are not edible!

PAPERWEIGHTS

Father's Day

This useful paperweight should be a great success as a gift on Father's Day. You will need a wooden doorknob or other small, but weighty, object to decorate. Choose a decoration that will suit his personality or hobbies; a garden-loving father would enjoy the gardening design and a DIY expert would like the woodworking tools! If he plays golf you could stick a real golf ball and tee onto the paperweight. Paint the paperweight in colours that suit the decoration - greens and browns for gardening or maybe blue, if your decoration has a watery theme.

You will need:

Wooden doorknob

Oven bake clay

Glue

Paint-brush

Paint

Varnish

Small decorations could be made from air hardening clay and painted if you did not have any oven bake clay.

1 Use coloured oven bake clay to make the vegetables. The carrots are made from tiny sausage shapes thinned at one end with a few green pieces stuck on as stalks. To make the cabbages begin with a few small ball shapes, and flatten them into leaf shapes. When you have made a few leaves press them, one by one, onto a small ball, until you have a hearty looking cabbage. Pumpkins are made from flattened ball shapes, and the tomatoes are small red ball shapes with tiny green stalks. The miniature basket came from a florist's shop, but you could make a basket from clay. Harden the vegetables in the oven according to the manufacturer's instructions. Paint the doorknob dark green. Use strong glue to attach the vegetables and basket to the doorknob.

2 When the glue has dried brighten up the paperweight with a little red paint and then varnish the whole item to give a professional finish.

3 The doorknob has been left unpainted for this carpenter's design. Make the miniature tools from oven bake clay, baked in the oven according to the manufacturer's instructions.

4 Use glue to attach the hardened tools to the doorknob and when the glue has dried, varnish the paperweight. For a golfing father, decorate the doorknob with a golf ball and tee.

Measurements

TEMPERATURE

Fahrenheit	Centigrade
250-300	120-150
300-350	150-175
350-375	175-190
375-400	190-200
400-425	200-220

LENGTH

cm	ins
2.5	1
5	2
7.6	3
10	4
12.7	5
15	6
17.7	7
20	8
22.8	9
25.4	10

WEIGHT

oz	grams
1	30
3	75
6	175
8	250

This is a Parragon Book
This edition published in 2002

Parragon
Queen Street House
4 Queen Street
Bath BA1 1HE, UK

9780752584034

Produced by Miles Kelly Publishing Ltd
This edition and cover design by Design Principals, Warminster

A copy of the British Library Cataloguing-in-Publication Data is available from the British Library.

ISBN 0-75258-403-0

Printed in China

THINGS TO MAKE AND DO

Vivienne Bolton

p